How to love yourself

ABRAHAM DOLLAR

HOW TO LOVE YOURSELF

It's Okay to Love Yourself

How to love yourself

Copyright ©2023 by Abraham Dollar

HOW TO LOVE YOURSELF
It's Ok to Love Yourself

ISBN: 9798850916381

Unless otherwise noted, all scripture quotations are from the King James Version of the Bible.

All rights reserved. No part of this publication may be reproduced, distributed, or transmitted in any form or by any electronic or mechanical means without written permission of the publisher except for brief quotations embodied in critical reviews and other non-commercial uses permitted by copyright law.

For ordering and further information, kindly write to the publisher

Published by

in the Republic of Ireland
zionhousesingapore@gmail.com

How to love yourself

TABLE OF CONTENTS

COPYRIGHT PAGE

ACKNOWLEDGEMENTS

DEDICATION

TABLE OF CONTENTS

INTRODUCTION

CHAPTER 1.......... Why Christians Struggle with Self-Love

CHAPTER 2.......... Setting Boundaries

CHAPTER 3.......... Prioritizing You

CHAPTER 4.......... Building Self-Esteem

CHAPTER 5.......... Overcoming Fear

How to love yourself

PERSONAL-ACKNOWLEDGEMENT

"I acknowledge that loving oneself is a vital and fundamental aspect of personal growth and development. It takes courage and self-awareness to accept ourselves for who we are and to embrace our strengths and weaknesses.

Self-love involves taking care of ourselves physically, mentally, and emotionally. It means setting healthy boundaries, prioritizing our needs, and treating ourselves with kindness and compassion.

I recognize that loving oneself is a journey, and it requires patience, practice, and persistence. It involves celebrating small successes and accepting setbacks as opportunities for growth and learning.

I acknowledge that learning how to love oneself is an ongoing process, and we can always improve and strive to become the best version of ourselves. It is a gift that we can give ourselves and an essential step towards living a fulfilling and meaningful life."

How to love yourself

DEDICATION

To all the brave souls who have struggled to find self-love and self-acceptance, this book is for you. Your journey toward self-love may have been tough, but it is important to remember that you are enough. May this book help you uncover the beauty and strength within yourself and guide you towards true self-love. Remember, you are worthy of love and deserve to give it to yourself.

How to love yourself

"Love your neighbour AS you love yourself"

"The second is this: 'You shall love your neighbour as yourself.' There is no other commandment greater than these."
(Mark 12:31)
"And a second is like it: You shall love your neighbour as yourself."
(Matthew 22:39)
"You shall not take vengeance or bear a grudge against the sons of your own people, but you shall love your neighbour as yourself: I am the Lord."
(Leviticus 19:18)
"For the whole law is fulfilled in one word: "You shall love your neighbour as yourself."
(Galatians 5:14)

How to love yourself

INTRODUCTION:

UNDERSTANDING THE IMPORTANCE OF SELF-LOVE

As Christians, we often focus on loving others and living a life of service to God and our neighbours. While these are important aspects of our faith, we often neglect to prioritize self-love and self-care and many of us may even view self-love as selfish or un-Christian.

However, self-love is an essential aspect of our spiritual and emotional well-being. It allows us to fully embrace our identity as children of God and to love others more deeply and authentically. Without self-love, we may struggle with feelings of worthlessness, guilt, and shame, and our ability to fulfil God's calling for our lives may be hindered.

This book aims to explore the concept of self-love in a Christian context and to offer practical strategies for cultivating self-love and self-care. We will begin by examining the biblical foundations of self-love and exploring what the Bible says about loving ourselves as well as others. We will then explore the reasons why Christians often struggle with self-love, including internalized shame and cultural messages that prioritize self-sacrifice over self-care.

How to love yourself

This book will also delve into the benefits of self-love for Christians, such as increased emotional resilience, greater capacity for compassion, and a deeper sense of connection with God and others. We will discuss practical strategies for cultivating self-love, including spiritual practices such as prayer and meditation, setting healthy boundaries, and building self-esteem.

This book is for any Christian who wants to deepen their relationship with God and themselves, and to live a life of greater emotional and spiritual health. I hope that it will be a valuable resource for readers as they embark on their own journey of self-love and self-care.

How to love yourself

BIBLICAL FOUNDATIONS OF SELF-LOVE:

WHAT THE BIBLE SAYS ABOUT SELF-LOVE AND SELF-CARE

Many Christians may be hesitant to embrace the concept of self-love, believing that it conflicts with the teachings of the Bible. However, the Bible has much to say about the importance of self-love and self-care.

One of the most well-known passages about self-love in the Bible is found in Mark 12:31, where Jesus teaches his disciples to *"love your neighbour as yourself."* This passage implies that self-love is a necessary foundation for loving others. In other words, we cannot love others well if we do not first love ourselves.

Another important passage about self-love is found in Psalm 139:14, which says, *"I praise you because I am fearfully and wonderfully made; your works are wonderful, I know that full well."* This passage reminds us that we are created in God's image and that we are inherently valuable and worthy of love and care.

The Bible also teaches that self-care is important for our physical, emotional, and spiritual health. In 1 Corinthians 6:19-20, Paul writes, *"Do you not know that your bodies are*

How to love yourself

temples of the Holy Spirit, who is in you, whom you have received from God? You are not your own; you were bought at a price. Therefore, honour God with your bodies." This passage emphasizes the importance of taking care of our physical bodies as a way of honouring God.

Additionally, the Bible teaches that self-care can be a form of worship. In Romans 12:1-2, Paul writes, *"Therefore, I urge you, brothers and sisters, in view of God's mercy, to offer your bodies as a living sacrifice, holy and pleasing to God—this is your true and proper worship. Do not conform to the pattern of this world, but be transformed by the renewing of your mind."* This passage suggests that taking care of our bodies and minds can be a way of offering ourselves to God as a living sacrifice.

Overall, the Bible affirms the importance of self-love and self-care as foundational aspects of our spiritual and emotional well-being. By embracing these concepts, we can deepen our relationship with God and others and live more fulfilling lives as Christians.

CHAPTER ONE

WHY CHRISTIANS STRUGGLE WITH SELF-LOVE

Exploring Common Barriers and Misconceptions

Despite the biblical foundations of self-love, many Christians struggle to embrace this concept due to common barriers and misconceptions. One of the main barriers is the belief that self-love is selfish or prideful. However, as discussed earlier, self-love is a necessary foundation for loving others well and honouring God with our bodies and minds.

Another common misconception is that self-love is the same as self-indulgence or self-centeredness. However, true self-love involves nurturing ourselves in healthy and balanced ways, rather than indulging in harmful behaviours or focusing solely on our own needs.

Many Christians also struggle with self-love due to negative self-talk or beliefs about themselves that are not aligned with God's truth. This can lead to feelings of shame, unworthiness, and self-doubt, making it difficult to embrace the idea of self-love.

16 REASONS WHY CHRISTIANS STRUGGLE WITH SELF-LOVE

1. Misconceptions about Self-Love:

Many Christians struggle with self-love because they view it as selfish or self-centred. To an extent, they believe that putting themselves first goes against the teachings of the Bible.

2. Guilt:

Some Christians struggle with self-love because they feel guilty for taking care of their own needs. They believe that they should be putting others first and taking time for themselves is selfish.

3. Perfectionism:

Many Christians hold themselves to high standards, and they believe that self-love is a form of pride or arrogance. They feel that they are not worthy of self-love unless they are perfect in every way.

4. Lack of Self-Worth:

Christians who struggle with low self-esteem or feelings of unworthiness may find it challenging to practice self-love. They are likely to believe that they are not deserving of love and care, or that they are inherently flawed.

5. Fear of Judgment:

Christians may worry about being judged by others for practicing self-love. They are likely afraid of appearing selfish or ungodly, and they may feel pressure to conform to societal or religious expectations.

How to love yourself

6. Religious Upbringing:

Some Christians may have grown up in environments where self-love was discouraged or even punished. They may have been taught that self-denial and sacrifice are essential virtues, and that self-love is a form of sin.

7. Negative Self-Talk:

Christians who struggle with negative self-talk may find it difficult to practice self-love. They may be plagued by feelings of self-doubt, self-criticism, or self-hatred.

8. Misunderstanding of God's Love:

Christians who struggle with self-love are likely not to fully understand God's unconditional love for them. They may believe that they have to earn God's love, or that their worth is based on their performance or achievements.

9. Lack of Boundaries:

Christians who struggle with self-love may have difficulty setting and enforcing healthy boundaries. They may feel obligated to say yes to every request or demand, even if it means sacrificing their own needs and desires.

10. Over-Identification with Others:

How to love yourself

Christians who struggle with self-love may have a strong sense of identity tied to others. They define themselves primarily by their relationships, roles, or responsibilities, rather than by their own needs and desires.

11. Fear of Self-Discovery:

Some Christians are afraid of exploring their thoughts, feelings, and desires. They are fearful that they will discover aspects of themselves that are ungodly or unacceptable.

12. Lack of Role Models:

Christians who struggle with self-love may not have had good role models for self-care and self-love. They may not have seen others in their lives practicing self-love, or they may not have had anyone to guide them in developing healthy self-love practices.

13. Misconceptions about Humility:

Christians may misunderstand the concept of humility and believe that self-love is incompatible with humility. They may believe that humility requires self-denial and self-sacrifice, and that self-love is a form of pride.

14. Fear of Failure:

Christians who struggle with self-love may be afraid of failing to live up to their expectations or the expectations of others. They may fear that if they prioritize their own needs and desires, they will disappoint others or fall short of their ideals.

15. Lack of Trust:

Christians who struggle with self-love may have difficulty trusting themselves or others. They believe that their own desires and needs are not valid, or they fear that others will take advantage of them if they prioritize their own needs.

16. Difficulty Expressing Emotions:

Christians who struggle with self-love may have difficulty expressing their own emotions and needs.

THE BENEFITS OF SELF-LOVE FOR CHRISTIANS: HOW IT CAN DEEPEN YOUR FAITH AND TRANSFORM YOUR LIFE

Despite these barriers and misconceptions, embracing self-love can have profound benefits for Christians. When we learn to love ourselves as God loves us, we deepen our relationship with Him and others and live more fulfilling lives.

Self-love can also help us to overcome negative self-talk and beliefs, and to embrace our identity as children of God. By forgiving ourselves and releasing resentment, we can experience God's unconditional love and grace, and deepen our faith.

PRACTICES FOR CULTIVATING SELF-LOVE:

Prayer, Meditation, and Other Spiritual Disciplines

Practices for cultivating self-love are essential for Christians to deepen their spiritual and emotional well-being. The following are some practices that can help cultivate self-love:

1. Prayer:

Prayer is one of the most powerful ways to cultivate self-love. It is a way to connect with God, to express our gratitude, to confess our sins, and to ask for guidance and help. Prayer also helps us to focus on God's love for us, and it reminds us that we are not alone. Praying for ourselves and others can also help us to develop a greater sense of compassion and empathy.

2. Meditation:

Meditation is another powerful practice for cultivating self-love. It is a way to quiet the mind, to focus on the present moment, and to connect with our inner selves. Christian meditation involves focusing on God's word, reflecting on His love for us, and allowing the Holy Spirit to guide us. Meditation helps us to become more aware of our thoughts and feelings, and it allows us to let go of negative beliefs and patterns.

3. Bible Study:

Studying the Bible is an essential practice for cultivating self-love. It is a way to connect with God's word, to learn more about His love for us and to deepen our understanding of His plan for our lives. Bible study helps us to develop a stronger faith and a greater sense of purpose.

4. Gratitude Journaling:

Gratitude journaling is a practice that involves writing down the things we are grateful for each day. This practice helps us to focus on the positive things in our lives, to develop a greater sense of appreciation, and to cultivate a more positive outlook. Gratitude journaling can also help us to recognize and overcome negative self-talk and beliefs.

5. Self-Care:

Self-care is a vital practice for cultivating self-love. It involves taking care of our physical, emotional, and spiritual needs. Examples of self-care practices include getting enough sleep, eating a healthy diet, exercising regularly, spending time with loved ones, engaging in hobbies and interests, and taking time to rest and relax. Practicing self-care helps us to build resilience, reduce stress, and nurture our overall well-being.

6. Forgiveness:

Forgiveness is a critical practice for cultivating self-love. It involves letting go of resentment, anger, and bitterness towards ourselves and others. Forgiveness helps us to release negative emotions and to embrace grace and love. Forgiving ourselves and others also helps us to deepen our relationship with God and to develop a greater sense of compassion and empathy.

Practicing self-love is essential for Christians to deepen their relationship with God, to cultivate a more positive outlook and to nurture their overall well-being. Through practices such as prayer, meditation, Bible study, gratitude journaling, self-care, and forgiveness, we can develop a greater sense of love, compassion, and empathy towards ourselves and others.

UNDERSTANDING YOUR IDENTITY IN CHRIST:

Embracing Your True Self as a Child of God

How to love yourself

One of the key aspects of self-love for Christians is embracing our identity as children of God. When we recognize that we are fearfully and wonderfully made in God's image, we can release feelings of shame and unworthiness, and embrace our true selves.

Forgiveness and Grace: Releasing Resentment and Accepting God's Unconditional Love

Forgiveness and grace are essential aspects of self-love for Christians. When we learn to forgive ourselves and others, we can release resentment and embrace God's unconditional love and grace.

CHAPTER TWO

SETTING BOUNDARIES

Respecting Yourself and Your Relationship with God and Others

How to love yourself

Setting boundaries is a necessary aspect of self-love for Christians. By respecting ourselves and our relationship with God and others, we can create healthy and balanced relationships and live fulfilling lives.

Prioritizing Your Needs: Finding Balance and Resilience in Your Spiritual Life. Prioritizing our needs is another important aspect of self-love for Christians. By finding balance and resilience in our spiritual lives, we can deepen our relationship with God and live more fulfilling lives.

Building Self-Esteem: Nurturing Confidence and Self-Worth Through Your Faith. Building self-esteem is an important aspect of self-love for Christians. By nurturing confidence and self-worth through our faith, we can overcome negative self-talk and beliefs, and embrace our true selves.

Connecting with God and Others: Building Healthy Relationships Through Self-Love. Connecting with God and others is an essential aspect of self-love for Christians. By building healthy and fulfilling relationships, we can deepen ours.

Personal Story: Share a story of a Christian who struggled with setting boundaries, such as feeling obligated to always say yes to others or feeling guilty for prioritizing their own needs. Practical Tip: Offer guidance on how readers can set healthy boundaries in their own lives, such as learning to say no, practicing assertiveness, or seeking support from trusted friends or mentors.

HERE ARE 50 WAYS TO SET BOUNDARIES:

1. Say "no" when you don't want to do something.

Saying "no" when you don't want to do something is an important part of setting boundaries and taking care of yourself. It allows you to prioritize your own needs and avoid overcommitting or feeling resentful. It can be difficult to say "no" at first, but with practice, it becomes easier and more empowering. Remember that it's okay to prioritize your own well-being and that saying "no" doesn't make you selfish or unkind.

2. Take time for yourself:

Taking time for yourself is crucial for cultivating self-love and preventing burnout. It allows you to recharge, reflect, and pursue activities that bring you joy and fulfilment. It's important to schedule regular "me time" into your routine and prioritize it as you would any other important appointment. Whether it's reading a book, taking a bath, or going for a walk, find activities that nourish your soul and make you feel renewed. Remember that taking time for yourself isn't selfish, it's necessary for your well-being.

3. Communicate your needs clearly:

Communicating your needs clearly is essential for setting healthy boundaries and fostering healthy relationships. It involves expressing your thoughts, feelings, and desires in a respectful and assertive manner. When you communicate your needs, you allow others to understand your perspective and help meet your needs. This can prevent misunderstandings, resentment, and conflict. Remember to be specific and concise when communicating your needs, and to listen actively to the needs of others as well.

4. Create personal space:

Creating personal space is crucial for establishing boundaries and promoting self-care. It involves setting aside physical, emotional, and mental space for yourself where you can retreat and recharge. This can include creating a designated area in your home for relaxation, taking breaks during the day to clear your mind, and setting limits on how much time you spend with certain people or in certain situations. Creating personal space allows you to focus on your own needs and well-being, and can help prevent burnout and stress.

5. Establish clear guidelines and expectations in relationships;

Establishing clear guidelines and expectations in relationships is essential for maintaining healthy boundaries and promoting mutual respect. This involves openly communicating your values, needs, and boundaries with others, and setting clear expectations for how you want to be treated. By establishing clear guidelines and expectations, you can prevent misunderstandings and build trust in your relationships. Remember to be respectful and considerate of the needs and expectations of others as well, and to revisit and adjust your guidelines and expectations as needed over time.

6. Identify your limits and communicate them to others:

Identifying your limits and communicating them to others is important for promoting self-care and setting boundaries. This involves recognizing your physical, emotional, and mental limits, and communicating them clearly to others. When you know your limits, you can prevent burnout and stress, and ensure that you have the energy and resources to meet your needs and responsibilities. Communicating your limits to others can also help prevent misunderstandings and promote healthy relationships. Remember to be honest and assertive when communicating your limits, and to listen actively to the limits of others as well.

7. Don't apologize for setting boundaries:

When setting boundaries, it is important not to apologize for doing so. Setting boundaries is a healthy and necessary part of self-care and establishing healthy relationships. It is important to assert your needs and values without feeling guilty or apologizing for doing so. Remember that setting boundaries is not a reflection of your worth or character and that it is okay to prioritize your own needs and well-being. By standing firm in your boundaries and not apologizing for them, you can establish a sense of confidence and assertiveness that will benefit you in all areas of your life.

8. Take responsibility for your own feelings and actions:

Taking responsibility for your own feelings and actions is a crucial aspect of setting boundaries

How to love yourself

and promoting self-love. This involves recognizing that you are responsible for your own emotional well-being and actions, and avoiding blaming others for your feelings or behaviour. By taking responsibility for your own emotions and actions, you can empower yourself to make positive changes in your life and relationships and avoid feeling victimized or helpless. Remember to communicate assertively and respectfully with others, and to take steps to address any negative patterns or behaviours that may be contributing to your feelings or actions. By taking responsibility for your feelings and actions, you can cultivate a sense of personal empowerment and resilience.

9. Be assertive:

Being assertive is an important part of setting boundaries and promoting self-love. It involves communicating your needs and preferences in a clear, respectful, and direct manner. Assertiveness can help you avoid passive or aggressive communication styles, and establish healthy boundaries and relationships. Remember to use "I" statements to express your thoughts and feelings, and to avoid blaming or attacking others. Be confident in your worth and values, and don't be afraid to assert your needs and boundaries when necessary. By being assertive, you can promote self-respect and positive relationships with others.

How to love yourself

10. Avoid people who consistently disrespect your boundaries
11. Don't feel guilty for saying no
12. Use "I" statements when expressing your needs and boundaries
13. Avoid overcommitting yourself
14. Prioritize your own needs
15. Don't take on other people's responsibilities
16. Take breaks when needed
17. Learn to say "yes" only when you truly want to
18. Avoid people who consistently violate your boundaries
19. Don't be afraid to ask for help or support
20. Don't allow others to guilt or shame you into doing things you don't want to do
21. Be clear and concise in your communication
22. Practice self-care regularly
23. Don't be afraid to seek professional help or counselling
24. Identify your triggers and set boundaries around them
25. Set consequences for boundary violations
26. Learn to forgive yourself for mistakes or slip-ups

How to love yourself

27. Surround yourself with people who respect your boundaries
28. Be consistent in enforcing your boundaries
29. Don't make exceptions to your boundaries for certain people
30. Don't engage in activities that compromise your boundaries
31. Set boundaries around social media and technology use
32. Set boundaries around work and career demands
33. Set boundaries around financial issues
34. Don't feel guilty for taking care of yourself
35. Practice self-compassion and self-forgiveness
36. Set boundaries around physical touch and intimacy
37. Don't be afraid to end toxic relationships
38. Take time to reflect on your boundaries and adjust them as needed
39. Set boundaries around your emotional needs
40. Don't be afraid to seek feedback from trusted friends or family members
41. Set boundaries around your time and schedule

42. Practice mindfulness to stay in touch with your needs and boundaries
43. Set boundaries around family dynamics and expectations
44. Avoid people who consistently drain your energy or resources
45. Set boundaries around communication methods (e.g. phone, email, text)
46. Don't be afraid to express your emotions and feelings
47. Set boundaries around social events and gatherings
48. Practice gratitude for the positive people and things in your life
49. Set boundaries around your personal values and beliefs
50. Don't be afraid to make changes and adjustments to your boundaries over time

EMBRACING YOUR IMPERFECTIONS: RECOGNIZING THAT YOU ARE A WORK IN PROGRESS

Embracing our imperfections is another important aspect of self-love for Christians. When we recognize that we are a work in

How to love yourself

progress, we can release the pressure to be perfect and embrace our humanity.

Embracing our imperfections is an integral part of self-love for Christians because it allows us to be vulnerable and authentic with ourselves and others. Recognizing that we are a work in progress means acknowledging that we are not perfect and that we make mistakes. It also means accepting ourselves for who we are, flaws and all.

One of the main reasons why many Christians struggle with embracing their imperfections is because of the belief that they need to be perfect to be accepted by God. This belief can lead to feelings of shame and guilt when we fall short of our own or others' expectations. However, the Bible teaches us that God's love is unconditional and that we are accepted and loved just as we are, imperfections and all.

When we embrace our imperfections, we can let go of the need to be perfect and focus on growth and improvement. We can learn from our mistakes and use them as opportunities for growth and self-reflection. Instead of beating ourselves up over our imperfections, we can show ourselves compassion and grace, just as God does.

How to love yourself

Embracing our imperfections also allows us to connect with others on a deeper level. When we share our struggles and vulnerabilities with others, it creates a sense of authenticity and trust that can strengthen our relationships. It also helps us to recognize that we are not alone in our imperfections and that others struggle with the same issues.

To embrace our imperfections, we can start by practicing self-compassion and self-forgiveness. We can remind ourselves that we are human and that making mistakes is a natural part of the learning and growing process. We can also surround ourselves with people who accept us for who we are and who support us in our growth and development.

Another way to embrace our imperfections is to focus on our strengths and positive qualities. By recognizing and celebrating our unique strengths and talents, we can build our self-confidence and self-esteem. We can also use our strengths to contribute to the world in meaningful ways.

Embracing our imperfections is an essential aspect of self-love for Christians. By recognizing that we are a work in progress, we can release the pressure to be perfect and focus on growth and self-improvement. We can also connect with

How to love yourself

others on a deeper level and celebrate our unique strengths and qualities.

CHAPTER THREE

PRIORITIZING YOU

Finding Balance and Resilience in Your Spiritual Life

How to love yourself

Prioritizing your needs is an important aspect of self-love and can help you find balance and resilience in your spiritual life. When you take care of yourself, you can better serve God and others.

UNDERSTANDING THE IMPORTANCE OF PRIORITIZING YOUR NEEDS

Why self-care is important and why it's not selfish to prioritize your own needs!

As a Christian, it can be easy to fall into the trap of believing that prioritizing our own needs is selfish or goes against the teachings of the Bible. However, it's important to recognize that self-care is not only beneficial for our own well-being, but it can also help us better serve others and fulfil our God-given purpose.

Jesus himself often took time for rest and solitude, recognizing the importance of caring for his own needs in order to carry out his ministry effectively. In Mark 6:31, it states, *"Then, because so many people were coming and going that they did not even have a chance to eat, he said to them, 'Come with me by yourselves to a quiet place and get some rest.'"*

In addition, 1 Corinthians 6:19-20 reminds us that our bodies are temples of the Holy Spirit, and therefore it's important to take care of them: *"Do you not know that your bodies are temples of the Holy Spirit, who is in you, whom you have received from God? You are not your own; you were bought at a price. Therefore, honour God with your bodies."*

Prioritizing our own needs doesn't mean neglecting our responsibilities or ignoring the needs of others. It simply means recognizing that we are also important and deserving of care and attention. When we take care of ourselves physically, emotionally, and spiritually, we are better equipped to handle the demands of daily life and serve others with love and compassion.

Prioritizing our needs as Christians is not selfish, but rather it is a necessary part of living a fulfilling and purposeful life in service to God and others.

IDENTIFYING YOUR PERSONAL NEEDS AND VALUES

Identifying your personal needs and values is a crucial step in prioritizing your needs and finding balance in your spiritual life. Many Christians struggle with the idea of prioritizing

How to love yourself

their own needs because they feel that it is selfish or goes against the idea of selflessness that is often emphasized in Christianity. However, it is important to remember that taking care of yourself and identifying your personal needs is not only important for your well-being but also for the well-being of those around you. When you prioritize your own needs, you are better able to serve and love others.

To begin identifying your personal needs and values, take some time to reflect on what brings you joy and what drains your energy. This could involve making a list of activities or experiences that bring you happiness, fulfilment, and a sense of purpose. It could also involve reflecting on the areas of your life that are causing you stress, anxiety, or exhaustion.

Next, consider what values are important to you. These may include values such as honesty, compassion, generosity, or faith. Identify which values are most important to you and how you can prioritize these values in your daily life.

As you identify your personal needs and values, it is important to remember that they may change over time. What brought you joy and fulfilment in the past may not be the same as what brings you joy and fulfilment now. It is okay to adjust your priorities and make changes as needed to ensure that you are taking care of yourself and living a life that is aligned with your values.

In addition to identifying your personal needs and values, it is important to take practical steps to prioritize these needs in your daily life. This may involve setting boundaries with others, learning to say "no" to activities or commitments that do not align with your priorities, and making time for self-care activities such as exercise, meditation, or spending time in nature.

Overall, identifying your personal needs and values is an important step in prioritizing your needs and finding balance in your spiritual life. By taking the time to reflect on what brings you joy and fulfilment and prioritizing these needs, you can live a more purposeful and fulfilling life while also being better equipped to serve and love others.

RECOGNIZING THE SIGNS OF BURNOUT AND NEGLECTING YOUR NEEDS

Recognizing the signs of burnout and neglecting your needs is an important step in prioritizing your needs as a Christian. Many people struggle with putting their own needs first and instead prioritize the needs of others, which can lead to burnout and neglect of one's well-being. It's important to recognize the signs of burnout and neglect in order to take proactive steps to prevent it.

Some common signs of burnout and neglect include feeling overwhelmed, exhausted, or irritable. You may also find yourself lacking motivation or feeling disconnected from the things that once brought you joy. Physical symptoms such as headaches, fatigue, or difficulty sleeping may also be present.

If you notice these signs, it's important to take action. This may involve setting aside time for yourself to recharge, seeking support from loved ones or a professional, and reassessing your priorities and commitments. Recognizing and addressing burnout and neglect of your needs can help you live a more balanced and fulfilling life, and ultimately deepen your faith as a Christian.

FINDING BALANCE IN YOUR SPIRITUAL LIFE

Finding balance in your spiritual life is essential to prioritizing your needs and maintaining overall wellness. Here are some practical tips to help readers find balance:

1. Prioritize spiritual disciplines:

How to love yourself

Make time for daily prayer, Bible study, and meditation. This could be in the morning, during a lunch break, or before bed. Find a time that works for you and make it a priority.

2. Set realistic goals:

Don't overwhelm yourself with unrealistic goals. Start small and gradually increase the amount of time you spend on spiritual disciplines. Setting achievable goals will help you stay motivated and avoid burnout.

3. Incorporate spirituality into daily life:

Look for ways to incorporate spiritual practices into your daily routine. This could include praying during your commute, reading a devotional during lunch break, or listening to worship music while doing home chores.

4. Schedule a regular time for rest or relaxation:

Make sure to schedule time for rest and relaxation. This could include taking a walk, practicing yoga, or reading a book. Taking time for yourself will help you recharge and feel more balanced.

5. Learn to say "no":

Don't be afraid to say "no" to commitments that may interfere with your spiritual life. Setting boundaries will help you prioritize your needs and make time for the things that matter most.

6. Seek support:

Surround yourself with supportive friends and family members who share your values and beliefs. Joining a small group or Bible study can also provide accountability and encouragement.

Finding balance in your spiritual life is an ongoing process. It requires self-awareness, discipline, and a willingness to make your spiritual health a priority. By following these practical tips, you can achieve greater balance in your spiritual life and experience greater overall wellness.

SETTING REALISTIC GOALS AND EXPECTATIONS FOR YOURSELF

Setting realistic goals and expectations is an important aspect of prioritizing your needs as a Christian. It can be easy to get caught up in the expectations of others, whether they are societal, familial, or even church-related. However, when we set unrealistic goals for

How to love yourself

ourselves, we risk burnout and neglecting our own needs.

To set realistic goals, it's important to first identify what is most important to us. This can involve reflecting on our personal values, priorities, and life goals. From there, we can begin to set goals that align with those values and priorities.

It's also important to consider our limitations and resources when setting goals. This could include considering our available time, energy levels, and financial resources. When we set goals that are too ambitious or unrealistic, we risk setting ourselves up for failure and disappointment.

Learning to say no is another important aspect of setting realistic goals and expectations. It can be tempting to take on every opportunity that comes our way, this can overwhelm one and lead to burnout. By learning to say no to commitments that do not align with our values or priorities, we can free up time and energy to focus on what is most important to us.

In summary, setting realistic goals and expectations is crucial for finding balance and prioritizing our needs as Christians. By identifying our values and priorities, considering

How to love yourself

our limitations and resources, and learning to say no, we can set ourselves up for success and avoid burnout.

MAKING TIME FOR SELF-CARE AND RELAXATION

Making time for self-care and relaxation is crucial for finding balance and resilience in your spiritual life. Here are some practical suggestions for prioritizing self-care and relaxation:

1. Schedule downtime:

Just as you would schedule appointments and meetings, schedule time for yourself to rest and recharge. This could be a regular weekly or monthly activity or a spontaneous break when you need it.

2. Engage in activities that bring joy and relaxation:

Think about activities that bring you joy and relaxation, such as reading a book, taking a bubble bath, going for a walk in nature, or practicing yoga. Make time for these activities regularly to recharge and rejuvenate.

3. Practice mindfulness:

How to love yourself

Mindfulness is the practice of being present and fully engaged at the moment. Take a few moments each day to focus on your breath and be fully present in the moment. This can help reduce stress and increase feelings of calm and well-being.

4. Get enough sleep:

Prioritize getting enough sleep each night to help your body and mind recharge. Create a bedtime routine that helps you wind down and relax before sleep.

5. Practice self-compassion:

Be kind to yourself and treat yourself with the same kindness and compassion that you would offer to a friend. Allow yourself to take breaks when needed and don't push yourself beyond your limits.

By prioritizing self-care and relaxation, you can recharge and build resilience, making it easier to balance your spiritual life with other aspects of your life.

BUILDING HEALTHY HABITS AND ROUTINES

How to love yourself

Building healthy habits and routines is an essential aspect of self-care and prioritizing your needs as a Christian. Here are some practical tips on how to build healthy habits and routines that support your well-being:

1. Start Small:

Begin by making small, manageable changes to your daily routine. This could include going for a short walk after dinner or taking a few minutes each morning to practice deep breathing or meditation.

2. Set Realistic Goals:

When setting goals for yourself, make sure they are realistic and achievable. Avoid setting lofty goals that are difficult to attain, as this can lead to frustration and disappointment.

3. Develop a Routine:

Establish a daily routine that works for you and your lifestyle. This could include waking up at the same time each day, scheduling regular meals, and setting aside time for exercise and relaxation.

4. Exercise Regularly:

Regular exercise is an essential part of building healthy habits and routines. Find an exercise

How to love yourself

routine that works for you, whether it's going for a run, attending a yoga class, or lifting weights.

5. Eat Well:

Eating a well-balanced, nutritious diet is crucial for maintaining good health. Focus on incorporating plenty of fruits, vegetables, whole grains, and lean protein into your diet.

6. Get Enough Sleep: Sleep is essential for your physical and mental health. Make sure to get enough sleep each night, ideally between seven and nine hours.

7. Practice Mindfulness:

Incorporate mindfulness practices into your daily routine, such as meditation, deep breathing, or yoga. These practices can help reduce stress, improve focus, and promote a sense of calm and well-being.

By incorporating these habits and routines into your daily life, you can support your overall well-being and prioritize your needs as a Christian. Remember, building healthy habits takes time and practice, so be patient and kind to yourself as you work towards your goals.

Seeking support and accountability from others

Seeking support and accountability from others can be an effective way to stay on track with building healthy habits and prioritizing your needs. Here are some ways to seek support and accountability from others:

1. Join a support group:

There are various support groups available, both online and offline, for different needs and interests. Joining a support group can help you connect with others who are going through similar experiences and provide you with a safe space to share your thoughts and feelings.

2. Find an accountability partner:

An accountability partner can be someone you trust, who can provide you with regular check-ins and support to help you stay on track with your goals. This could be a friend, family member, or a professional coach.

3. Seek professional support:

Seeking professional support from a therapist or counsellor can help you gain new insights and perspectives on your needs and priorities, and provide you with personalized guidance and support.

4. Attend group fitness classes:

Group fitness classes can be a fun way to exercise and connect with others who share similar interests. This can provide you with a sense of community and motivation to maintain a regular exercise routine.

5. Connect with like-minded individuals:

Connecting with others who share similar values and interests can provide you with a sense of belonging and support in your journey of self-care and prioritizing your needs. This could involve joining a faith-based group, volunteering for a cause you care about, or participating in a hobby group.

Remember, seeking support and accountability from others is not a sign of weakness but rather a sign of strength and courage to prioritize your well-being.

CULTIVATING RESILIENCE IN THE FACE OF CHALLENGES AND SETBACKS

How to love yourself

Cultivating resilience in the face of challenges and setbacks is an important aspect of prioritizing your needs in your spiritual life. As Christians, we can draw on the strength of our faith and rely on God's promises to help us through difficult times.

One way to cultivate resilience is by practicing self-compassion. This means treating ourselves with kindness and understanding, even when we make mistakes or face challenges. As it says in Colossians 3:12, *"Therefore, as God's chosen people, holy and dearly loved, clothe yourselves with compassion, kindness, humility, gentleness and patience."* We can extend this same compassion and kindness to ourselves.

Another important aspect of resilience is learning from setbacks. In Romans 8:28, it says, *"And we know that in all things God works for the good of those who love him, who have been called according to his purpose."* Even in difficult times, God can use our struggles to teach us important lessons and help us grow stronger. By reflecting on our experiences and learning from them, we can build resilience and become more prepared for future challenges.

Resilience enables us to bounce back from challenges and setbacks, and to stay grounded and focused even in difficult circumstances.

How to love yourself

Here are some practical tips for cultivating resilience:

- **Practice self-compassion:**

When we are facing challenges, it's easy to be hard on ourselves and blame ourselves for our problems. But practicing self-compassion means treating ourselves with the same kindness and understanding that we would offer to a close friend. This can involve reminding ourselves that we are only human and that it's okay to make mistakes or face difficulties.

- **Learn from setbacks:**

Instead of seeing setbacks as failures, try to view them as opportunities for growth and learning. Reflect on what went wrong and what you can do differently in the future. This can help you develop resilience and adapt to new challenges more easily.

- **Stay connected:**

Maintaining strong relationships with friends, family, and community can be an important source of support and resilience. Try to stay connected with people who uplift you and make you feel supported, even if it's just through phone calls or video chats.

How to love yourself

- **Practice mindfulness:**

Mindfulness can help us stay grounded and focused even in difficult circumstances. Take time to notice your thoughts and feelings without judging them, and try to stay present in the moment rather than getting lost in worries about the future or regrets about the past.

Seeking help when needed is also crucial for cultivating resilience. As it says in Proverbs 15:22, *"Plans fail for lack of counsel, but with many advisers they succeed."* By seeking guidance and support from others, whether through friends, family, or professional help, we can build a network of support and strengthen our resilience.

TRUSTING IN GOD'S PLAN FOR YOUR LIFE WHILE PRIORITIZING YOUR NEEDS

Trusting in God's plan for your life while prioritizing your needs can be a challenging task for Christians. However, it is essential to remember that God desires us to take care of ourselves while trusting in His ultimate plan for our lives. Proverbs 3:5-6 reminds us to *"Trust in the Lord with all your heart and lean not on your own understanding; in all your ways submit to him, and he will make your paths straight."*

How to love yourself

Prayer and reflection are important tools in seeking guidance and direction from God. By setting aside time for prayer and reflection, we can gain clarity on our personal needs and desires while also seeking God's will for our lives. Philippians 4:6-7 encourages us to "not be anxious about anything, but in every situation, by prayer and petition, with thanksgiving, present your requests to God. And the peace of God, which transcends all understanding, will guard your hearts and your minds in Christ Jesus."

It is also important to remember that seeking help from others, whether through counselling or support groups, is not a sign of weakness but a step towards growth and resilience. As 1 Thessalonians 5:11 says, "Therefore encourage one another and build each other up, just as in fact you are doing."

By trusting in God's plan for our lives and prioritizing our own needs through prayer, reflection, and seeking help from others, we can cultivate a sense of resilience and strength that enables us to navigate life's challenges with grace and faith.

CHAPTER FOUR

BUILDING SELF-ESTEEM

How to love yourself

Building self-esteem is essential for living a fulfilling and satisfying life. As a Christian, nurturing confidence and self-worth through faith is vital in cultivating a healthy sense of self-esteem. Here are some ways to nurture confidence and self-worth through your faith:

- **Embrace your identity in Christ:**

Recognize that your worth comes from being a child of God and not from external sources such as achievements or material possessions. 2 Corinthians 5:17 states, *"Therefore, if anyone is in Christ, the new creation has come: The old has gone, the new is here!"*

- **Focus on positive self-talk:**

Pay attention to the way you talk to yourself and work to replace negative self-talk with positive affirmations based on biblical truths. For example, remind yourself that you are fearfully and wonderfully made (Psalm 139:14).

Focusing on positive self-talk is a powerful tool for building self-esteem and nurturing confidence in oneself. Oftentimes, negative self-talk can become a habit, and we may not even realize the impact it is having on our self-esteem. Negative self-talk can include thoughts

How to love yourself

and beliefs such as "I'm not good enough," "I'm a failure," or "I'm not worthy of love or success."

To counteract these negative beliefs, it's important to pay attention to the way we talk to ourselves and work to replace negative self-talk with positive affirmations based on biblical truths. One example of a biblical truth that can be used for positive self-talk is the verse from Psalm 139:14, which says, *"I praise you because I am fearfully and wonderfully made; your works are wonderful, I know that full well."* This verse reminds us that we are all uniquely and wonderfully made by God, and that we are worthy of love and respect simply because we exist.

Other examples of positive affirmations based on biblical truth might include reminding ourselves that we are loved by God (John 3:16), that we are forgiven (1 John 1:9), and that we are valuable in God's eyes (Matthew 10:31). By focusing on these positive affirmations and repeating them to ourselves regularly, we can begin to retrain our minds and build our self-esteem.

It's important to note that building self-esteem through positive self-talk is not a quick fix. It takes time and consistent effort to reprogram our minds and build new habits. However, with patience, perseverance, and a reliance on God's grace and strength, we can learn to replace negative self-talk with positive affirmations, and in turn, nurture confidence and self-worth through our faith.

FORGIVE YOURSELF AND OTHERS

Holding onto grudges and past mistakes can damage self-esteem. As a Christian, forgiveness is a central tenet of our faith. Forgiving yourself and others can free you from negative feelings and promote healthy self-esteem.

As a Christian, forgiveness is a fundamental aspect of our faith. Forgiveness is not only necessary for our spiritual well-being, but it also plays a crucial role in promoting healthy self-esteem. When we forgive ourselves and others, we release ourselves from the burden of holding onto grudges and negative feelings that can damage our self-worth.

The Bible teaches us to forgive others, just as God has forgiven us. In Colossians 3:13, it says, "Bear with each other and forgive one another if any of you has a grievance against someone. Forgive as the Lord forgave you." This verse reminds us that God has forgiven us, and we should also extend that forgiveness to others.

How to love yourself

Forgiving ourselves can be just as challenging as forgiving others. However, it is necessary to recognize that we all make mistakes and fall short of God's standards. We must learn to forgive ourselves and move forward in grace. In Psalm 103:12, it says, *"As far as the east is from the west, so far has he removed our transgressions from us."* This verse reminds us that God has forgiven us and removed our sins from us.

Forgiveness is a crucial aspect of our faith that promotes healthy self-esteem. By forgiving ourselves and others, we free ourselves from the burden of negative feelings and promote a positive self-image. Through forgiveness, we can nurture our confidence and self-worth in Christ.

SERVE OTHERS

Serving others can give you a sense of purpose and value. Jesus set an example of servant leadership, and when we serve others, we reflect His character.

Serving others is a key aspect of the Christian faith and can have a profound impact on our self-esteem. When we serve others, we not only make a positive impact on their lives but also gain a sense of purpose and fulfilment.

How to love yourself

In Matthew 20:28, Jesus said, *"the Son of Man came not to be served but to serve, and to give his life as a ransom for many."* He modelled servant leadership and emphasized the importance of serving others. Similarly, in Galatians 5:13, Paul wrote, *"serve one another in love."*

When we serve others, we not only fulfil the command to love our neighbours as ourselves (Mark 12:31), but also gain a sense of purpose and value. In 1 Peter 4:10-11, we are reminded that each of us has been given a gift to use to serve others: *"Each of you should use whatever gift you have received to serve others, as faithful stewards of God's grace in its various forms."*

Serving others can take many forms, such as volunteering at a local food bank, helping a neighbour with yard work, or even simply offering a kind word to someone who is struggling. As we serve others, we can gain a greater appreciation for our own strengths and abilities, which can boost our self-esteem.

Serving others is an important aspect of the Christian faith and can have a positive impact on our self-esteem. By serving others, we fulfil Jesus' call to love our neighbours, gain a sense of purpose and fulfilment, and appreciate our own strengths and abilities.

PRACTICE GRATITUDE

Focusing on what you are grateful for can help shift your focus away from negative self-talk and increase self-esteem. Recognize the blessings in your life and give thanks to God.

Practicing gratitude is a powerful way to increase self-esteem and foster a positive mindset. It involves intentionally focusing on the things in our lives that we are thankful for, no matter how small they may seem. As Christians, we can practice gratitude by recognizing the many blessings that God has given us and expressing our thankfulness to Him.

The Bible teaches us to give thanks in all circumstances, not just when things are going well. In **1 Thessalonians 5:18, it says, *"give thanks in all circumstances; for this is God's will for you in Christ Jesus."*** This verse reminds us that even in difficult times, we can find something to be thankful for.

When we practice gratitude, we also shift our focus away from our problems and onto the positive aspects of our lives. **Philippians 4:8 says, *"Finally, brothers and sisters, whatever is true, whatever is noble, whatever is right, whatever is pure,***

How to love yourself

whatever is lovely, whatever is admirable—if anything is excellent or praiseworthy—think about such things." By focusing on the good things in our lives, we can foster a positive mindset and increase our self-esteem.

Practicing gratitude can take many forms, such as keeping a gratitude journal, writing thank-you notes to those who have helped us, or simply taking a few moments each day to reflect on the blessings in our lives. By intentionally cultivating a grateful attitude, we can increase our self-esteem and strengthen our faith.

SURROUND YOURSELF WITH POSITIVE INFLUENCES

Spend time with people who encourage and support you. Look for positive role models and mentors who can help you grow in your faith and self-esteem.

Surrounding yourself with positive influences can have a significant impact on your self-esteem. As a Christian, it's essential to surround yourself with people who uplift and encourage you, and who share similar values and beliefs. The Bible tells us in Proverbs 13:20, *"Walk with the wise and become wise, for a companion of fools suffers harm."*

How to love yourself

In addition to seeking out positive relationships, it's also important to guard against negative influences. In 1 Corinthians 15:33, we are reminded, *"Do not be misled: 'Bad company corrupts good character.'"* Spending time with those who criticize, gossip, or undermine your self-worth can be detrimental to your self-esteem.

When you surround yourself with positive influences, you can gain perspective, receive wise counsel, and find encouragement. Proverbs 27:17 says, *"As iron sharpens iron, so one person sharpens another."* Having positive role models and mentors can help sharpen you spiritually and emotionally, leading to greater confidence and self-worth.

Consider joining a Christian small group or Bible study to connect with like-minded individuals and build positive relationships. Seek out mentors in your church community or through online resources. By surrounding yourself with positive influences, you can nurture your self-esteem and grow in your faith.

TAKE CARE OF YOURSELF

How to love yourself

Prioritize self-care by taking care of your physical, emotional, and spiritual health. This could include regular exercise, healthy eating, getting enough sleep, and engaging in spiritual practices like prayer and meditation.

Taking care of oneself is important for overall well-being, and as Christians, we are called to honour and respect the body that God has given us. In **1 Corinthians 6:19-20,** *it says, "Do you not know that your bodies are temples of the Holy Spirit, who is in you, whom you have received from God? You are not your own; you were bought at a price. Therefore, honour God with your bodies."*

One way to take care of oneself is through regular exercise. **1 Timothy 4:8 states,** *"For physical training is of some value, but godliness has value for all things, holding promise for both the present life and the life to come."* Engaging in regular physical activity not only helps keep our bodies healthy, but it also releases endorphins, which can improve mood and reduce stress.

Eating a healthy, balanced diet is also important for physical and emotional well-being. In **Proverbs 25:16, it says,** *"If you find honey, eat just enough—too much of it, and you will vomit."* The verse highlights the importance of balance and moderation in our food choices.

How to love yourself

Eating too much or too little can lead to physical and emotional health issues.

Getting enough rest and sleep is also crucial for overall health. In **Psalm 127:2, it says, *"In vain you rise early and stay up late, toiling for food to eat—for he grants sleep to those he loves."*** God desires for us to rest and rejuvenate our bodies, and lack of sleep can have negative effects on our physical and emotional health.

Lastly, engaging in spiritual practices like prayer, meditation, and reading the Bible can help us connect with God and find inner peace.

"Do not be anxious about anything, but in every situation, by prayer and petition, with thanksgiving, present your requests to God. And the peace of God, which transcends all understanding, will guard your hearts and your minds in Christ Jesus." Philippians 4:6-7

Overall, taking care of oneself is important for physical, emotional, and spiritual well-being, and it is a way to honour and respect the body that God has given us.

By nurturing confidence and self-worth through faith, you can build healthy self-esteem and live a more fulfilling life. Remember that your worth

How to love yourself

comes from being a child of God, and He loves you unconditionally.

CHAPTER FIVE

Overcoming Fear

Trusting in God and Stepping Out in Faith

How to love yourself

As a Christian, overcoming fear means relying on God's strength, power, and faithfulness to face and conquer any fears or anxieties that we may have. It involves developing trust in God's promises and sovereignty, and learning to surrender our fears and anxieties to Him through prayer and reliance on His guidance. It also means identifying and confronting the root causes of our fears, and stepping out of our comfort zones with God's guidance and support. Ultimately, overcoming fear as a Christian means finding courage, peace, and rest in God's love and protection, even in the midst of trouble or uncertainty.

Fear is a common experience for many people, but it doesn't have to control our lives. As Christians, we have a unique resource for dealing with fear - our faith in God. Here are some key ideas and Bible verses that can help us overcome fear and step out in faith.

UNDERSTANDING THE NATURE OF FEAR AND ITS EFFECTS ON OUR LIVES

2 Timothy 1:7 says, **"For God gave us a spirit not of fear but of power and love and self-control."** Fear can be a powerful force in our lives, but it doesn't come from God. When we allow fear to control us, we give up our power

and our ability to love and exercise self-control. By understanding that fear is not from God, we can start to take steps to overcome it.

Additionally, Psalm 34:4 states, *"I sought the Lord, and he answered me; he delivered me from all my fears."* This verse reminds us that God is always available to help us overcome our fears. We don't have to face them alone, and we can trust that God will answer our prayers for help and deliver us from our fears.

Furthermore, Proverbs 29:25 warns us, "**Fear of man will prove to be a snare, but whoever trusts in the Lord is kept safe.**" Fear of what others may think or do can be a trap that keeps us from living the life God has for us. But when we trust in the Lord and His plans for us, we can be kept safe and secure.

Overall, understanding the nature of fear and its effects on our lives involves recognizing that it is not from God, seeking His help and deliverance, and trusting in Him instead of giving in to fear.

DEVELOPING TRUST IN GOD'S FAITHFULNESS AND SOVEREIGNTY

Proverbs 3:5-6 says, *"Trust in the Lord with all your heart, and do not lean on your own understanding. In all your ways*

How to love yourself

acknowledge him, and he will make straight your paths." Trusting in God's faithfulness and sovereignty means recognizing that He is in control, even when things seem uncertain or scary. By acknowledging God in all our ways and trusting in His guidance, we can have confidence that He will lead us on the right path.

Psalm 20:7 also reminds us, *"Some trust in chariots and some in horses, but we trust in the name of the Lord our God."* When we place our trust in God instead of our own abilities or worldly things, we can have a firm foundation that will not be shaken. Additionally, Hebrews 13:8 tells us that *"Jesus Christ is the same yesterday, today, and forever."* This means that God's faithfulness and sovereignty are unchanging and reliable, and we can trust in Him to always be with us and guide us through any situation.

Developing trust in God's faithfulness and sovereignty also involves having faith in His promises. Romans 8:28 assures us that *"we know that for those who love God all things work together for good, for those who are called according to his purpose."* Even when we don't understand what is happening, we can trust that God is working everything together for our good and His glory. Jeremiah 29:11 also reminds us of God's good plans for our lives:

How to love yourself

"For I know the plans I have for you, declares the Lord, plans for welfare and not for evil, to give you a future and a hope." Trusting in God's faithfulness and sovereignty means believing in His promises and having faith that He will fulfil them.

TRUSTING IN GOD'S PROTECTION AND DELIVERANCE IN TIMES OF TROUBLE

Trusting in God's protection and deliverance in times of trouble can help us overcome fear and anxiety. Psalm 27:1 says, *"The Lord is my light and my salvation—whom shall I fear? The Lord is the stronghold of my life—of whom shall I be afraid?"* This verse reminds us that God is our protector and that we can trust Him to deliver us from any trouble we may face.

When we face difficult situations, it's easy to become overwhelmed with fear and anxiety. However, if we focus on God's promises and His faithfulness, we can find comfort and strength to face our fears. God is always with us, and He promises to be our stronghold and our refuge in times of trouble.

Trusting in God's protection and deliverance requires a deep faith and a willingness to surrender our fears and anxieties to Him. It requires us to acknowledge that we cannot control everything in our lives and that we need God's help to overcome our fears. When we trust in God's protection and deliverance, we can find peace in the midst of our fears and know that God is always with us, protecting and guiding us.

Trusting in God's protection and deliverance in times of trouble is essential for overcoming fear and anxiety. As we turn to God and place our trust in Him, we can find the strength and courage to face our fears and overcome them. Let us hold onto Psalm 27:1 and trust that God will always be our light, salvation, and stronghold.

FINDING COURAGE THROUGH PRAYER AND RELIANCE ON GOD

Joshua 1:9 says, "Have I not commanded you? Be strong and courageous. Do not be frightened, and do not be dismayed, for the Lord your God is with you wherever you go." God's presence with us can give us the courage to face our fears. We can ask Him for help through prayer and rely on His strength to give us the courage we need.

Additionally, Philippians 4:13 says, "I can do all things through him who strengthens me." This verse reminds us that we can find courage and strength through Christ. We can turn to Him in prayer and ask for His help to overcome our fears. As we rely on Him, we can find the courage to face whatever challenges come our way.

IDENTIFYING AND CONFRONTING THE ROOT CAUSES OF FEAR

Psalm 34:4 says, *"I sought the Lord, and he answered me and delivered me from all my fears."* Sometimes, fear is a symptom of deeper issues that we need to address. By seeking the Lord and asking Him to help us identify the root causes of our fear, we can take steps to address those issues and find freedom from fear.

HERE ARE 10 COMMON ROOT CAUSES OF FEAR

1. **Lack of trust in God:** "When I am afraid, I put my trust in you. In God, whose word I praise, in God I trust; I shall not be afraid. What can flesh do to me?" Psalm 56:3-4
2. **Trauma or past experiences**: "Remember not the former things, nor consider the

things of old. Behold, I am doing a new thing; now it springs forth, do you not perceive it? I will make a way in the wilderness and rivers in the desert." Isaiah 43:18-19
3. **Fear of failure:** "I can do all things through him who strengthens me." Philippians 4:13
4. **Fear of rejection:** "What then shall we say to these things? If God is for us, who can be against us?" Romans 8:31
5. **Fear of the unknown:** "Trust in the Lord with all your heart, and do not lean on your own understanding. In all your ways acknowledge him, and he will make straight your paths." Proverbs 3:5-6
6. **Fear of death:** "O death, where is your victory? O death, where is your sting? The sting of death is sin, and the power of sin is the law. But thanks be to God, who gives us the victory through our Lord Jesus Christ." 1 Corinthians 15:55-57
7. **Fear of inadequacy:** "But he said to me, 'My grace is sufficient for you, for my power is made perfect in weakness.' Therefore I will boast all the more gladly of my weaknesses, so that the power of Christ may rest upon me." 2 Corinthians 12:9
8. **Fear of loss:** "Even though I walk through the valley of the shadow of death, I will

fear no evil, for you are with me; your rod and your staff, they comfort me." Psalm 23:4
9. **Fear of change:** "Behold, I am doing a new thing; now it springs forth, do you not perceive it? I will make a way in the wilderness and rivers in the desert." Isaiah 43:19
10. **Fear of the future:** "For I know the plans I have for you, declares the Lord, plans for welfare and not for evil, to give you a future and a hope." Jeremiah 29:11

STEPPING OUT OF COMFORT ZONES AND TAKING RISKS WITH GOD'S GUIDANCE

Isaiah 41:10 says, "Fear not, for I am with you; be not dismayed, for I am your God; I will strengthen you, I will help you, I will uphold you with my righteous right hand." Stepping out of our comfort zones and taking risks can be scary, but with God's guidance and strength, we can do it. We can trust that He will be with us every step of the way.

How to love yourself

13 WAYS OF STEPPING OUT OF COMFORT ZONES AND TAKING RISKS WITH GOD'S GUIDANCE:

1. Trust in God's plans:

"The heart of man plans his way, but the Lord establishes his steps." We can trust that God has a plan for our lives and step out in faith. Proverbs 16:9

2. Listen for God's voice:

"And your ears shall hear a word behind you, saying, 'This is the way, walk in it,' when you turn to the right or when you turn to the left." Isaiah 30:21 We can listen for God's guidance and follow His lead.

3. Surrender to God's will:

"In all your ways acknowledge him, and he will make straight your paths." Proverbs 3:6 We can surrender our plans and desires to God and trust that He will guide us in the right direction.

4. Seek wise counsel:

"Without counsel plans fail, but with many advisers they succeed." Proverbs 15:22 We can seek the advice of wise, Godly people to help us make decisions.

How to love yourself

5. Step out in faith:

"Now faith is the assurance of things hoped for, the conviction of things not seen." Hebrews 11:1 We can step out in faith, even when we don't know the outcome.

6. Embrace discomfort:

"Count it all joy, my brothers, when you meet trials of various kinds, for you know that the testing of your faith produces steadfastness." James 1:2-3 We can embrace discomfort and trials, knowing that they can build our character and faith.

7. Pray for courage:

"I can do all things through him who strengthens me." Philippians 4:13 We can pray for courage and strength to step out of our comfort zones.

8. Focus on God's power:

"But he said to me, 'My grace is sufficient for you, for my power is made perfect in weakness.'" We can focus on God's power rather than our own weaknesses and limitations.

9. Believe in God's provision:

How to love yourself

"Therefore do not be anxious, saying, 'What shall we eat?' or 'What shall we drink?' or 'What shall we wear?' For the Gentiles seek after all these things, and your heavenly Father knows that you need them all. But seek first the kingdom of God and his righteousness, and all these things will be added to you." Matthew 6:31-33 We can trust that God will provide for our needs as we seek to follow Him.

10. **Take small steps:**

"For the righteous falls seven times and rises again." Proverbs 24:16a We can take small steps out of our comfort zones and learn from our mistakes.

11. **Persevere through challenges:**

"Blessed is the man who remains steadfast under trial, for when he has stood the test he will receive the crown of life, which God has promised to those who love him." James 1:12 We can persevere through challenges, knowing that our faith will be strengthened.

12. **Lean on God's grace:**

"For by grace you have been saved through faith. And this is not your own doing; it is the gift of God, not a result of works, so that no one may boast." Ephesians 2:8-9 We can lean on

How to love yourself

God's grace and trust that He will guide us through any situation.

13. Remember God's faithfulness:

"The Lord makes firm the steps of the one who delights in him; though he may stumble, he will not fall, for the Lord upholds him with his hand." - Psalm 37:23-24

Remembering God's faithfulness in the past can give us confidence and trust in Him for the future. We can trust that He will make our paths straight and uphold us with His hand, even when we stumble or face obstacles. By delighting in Him and seeking His guidance, we can have assurance that He is faithful and trustworthy.

OVERCOMING ANXIETY THROUGH PEACE AND REST IN GOD

"Do not be anxious about anything, but in everything by prayer and supplication with thanksgiving let your requests be made known to God. And the peace of God, which surpasses all understanding, will guard your hearts and your minds in Christ Jesus."
-Philippians 4:6-7 Anxiety is a form of fear that

can be especially debilitating. But by bringing our fears and anxieties to God in prayer and focusing on His peace, we can find rest and freedom from anxiety.

Here are some possible subtopics for overcoming anxiety through peace and rest in God, with corresponding scriptures:

Surrendering control to God:

Recognizing that we are not in control and trusting in God's plan for our lives can bring peace and calmness to our anxious hearts. (Proverbs 3:5-6, Matthew 6:25-34)

Practicing gratitude:

Focusing on the blessings in our lives and expressing gratitude can shift our perspective from anxiety to peace. (Philippians 4:6, Psalm 107:8-9)

Meditating on God's Word:

Filling our minds with God's promises and truths can replace anxious thoughts with peace and hope. (Isaiah 26:3, Psalm 119:165)

Seeking professional help:

While prayer and reliance on God are essential in overcoming anxiety, seeking help from mental health professionals can also be a wise step

How to love yourself

towards healing. (Proverbs 15:22, James 5:14-15)

Practicing self-care:

Taking care of our physical, emotional, and spiritual needs can help reduce anxiety and promote overall well-being. (1 Corinthians 6:19-20, Mark 6:31)

Surrendering to God's timing:

Trusting in God's timing and plan can help us let go of anxious thoughts and find peace in the present moment. (Ecclesiastes 3:1-8, Psalm 31:15)

Surrounding ourselves with positive influences:

Spending time with people who encourage and support us can help us feel less anxious and more at peace. (Proverbs 13:20, Romans 12:15)

RECOGNIZING THE POWER OF GOD'S LOVE TO CAST OUT FEAR

1 John 4:18 says, **"There is no fear in love, but perfect love casts out fear. For fear has to do with punishment, and whoever fears has not been perfected in love."** God's perfect love for us can overcome all fear. By recognizing

How to love yourself

that we are loved by God and allowing His love to fill us, we can find freedom from fear.

Here are some ways of recognizing the power of God's love to cast out fear with corresponding scriptures:

- **Meditate on God's love:**

Psalm 48:9 says, "We ponder your steadfast love, O God, in the midst of your temple." Take time to meditate on God's love for you and let it fill your heart.

- **Study God's Word:**

2 Timothy 3:16-17 says, "All Scripture is breathed out by God and profitable for teaching, for reproof, for correction, and for training in righteousness, that the man of God may be complete, equipped for every good work." Studying God's Word can help us understand His love and overcome fear.

- **Surrender to God's will:**

Romans 8:28 says, "And we know that for those who love God all things work together for good, for those who are called according to his purpose." Trusting in God's plan for our lives and surrendering to His will can give us peace and freedom from fear.

- **Focus on God's promises:**

How to love yourself

Isaiah 41:10 says, "Fear not, for I am with you; be not dismayed, for I am your God; I will strengthen you, I will help you, I will uphold you with my righteous right hand." Trusting in God's promises can help us overcome fear and anxiety.

- **Experience God's love through community:**

1 John 4:12 says, "No one has ever seen God; if we love one another, God abides in us and his love is perfected in us." Being part of a community of believers can help us experience God's love and overcome fear through the support and encouragement of others.

How to love yourself

THE SALVATION MESSAGE

4 STEPS TO SALVATION.

Dear Friend,

I am so grateful to God for the opportunity He has granted us to meet through this book. I understand how difficult it may be for you to give your life to God.

Everyone knows their weak point. In the closet try and identify your weaknesses and work on them immediately. Don't wait for tomorrow because it may be too late. Face that problem now and claim your miracles. Funny enough our sin is usually what makes us to come short of the glory of God.

I am using myself as an example because today I have endless testimonies.

Salvation is the only way to enjoy the work of the almighty in totality. If you give your life to Jesus Christ and accept Him as your lord and personal saviour, it is the fastest and surest key to stepping into that "wonderful Destiny" He has in store for you. Are you tired of the things not working out for you? Are you tired of always having your own way? Why not surrender to Jesus today as you take these steps of faith...

STEP 1   CONFESS YOUR SINS

How to love yourself

'He that covereth his sins shall not prosper: but whoso confesseth and forsaketh them shall have mercy.' (Proverbs 28:13).

STEP 2 : ASK GOD TO FORGIVE YOU

'If we confess our sins, he is faithful and just to forgive us our sins, and to cleanse us from all unrighteousness.' (1 John 1:9).

STEP 3: INVITE HIM INTO YOUR LIFE

'Behold, I stand at the door, and knock: if any man hear my voice, and open the door, I will come to him, and will sup with him, and he with me.' (Rev. 3:20).

STEP 4 : RECEIVE HIM BY FAITH

'But as many as received him, to them gave HE power to become the sons of God, even to them that believe on his name.' (John 1:12).

Please pray with me....

Dear Lord JESUS, today I come to you as a sinner, I confess my sins, forgive me and cleanse me.

Wash me with your precious blood. I invite you into my life today, even as I make you my personal Lord and SAVIOUR. I receive the gift of eternal life. I am BORN AGAIN. Thank you JESUS for accepting me and saving me now. Amen.

How to love yourself

WELCOME TO GOD'S FAMILY.

As you are aware, every plant needs water for growth and vitality, without which it would die. As a fresh Christian, you need spiritual nutrients to keep you alive, full of vitality and victory. You need to be where like-minded people are.

You may say 'I don't want to go to Church because I don't want to be known as such a church person' but do you know that a student is not identified as such unless he is part of a class? A child cannot claim to be a member of a family if he is not part of it. So also, you need to be around Christians if you say you are one, and the best place to find them is in Church.

As LONG as the branch stays connected to the tree, it will stay alive. As long as the baby stays close to the mother, he will have what to eat. As long as you stay connected to other believers, you will not be tempted to fall back into sin, deprivation and discouragement.

Join a Bible-believing church where you can grow in the word of God as you listen to quality teachings; learn how to pray; and get to meet with other Christians who can encourage you.

BACK TO THE BEGINNING

You are now born again. What does this mean? How will it change your life?

What does it mean to receive JESUS?

How to love yourself

You have made peace with GOD. You have a new relationship with GOD, your father, reconciled by the blood of JESUS. (John 10:10).

Like the prodigal son, you have finally come home (Luke 15:24).

You have been saved from sin, addiction, fear, guilt and shame. On the cross, JESUS paid it all for you (Romans 8:1).

You are now a member of the largest gathering on earth- the people of GOD

(1 Peter 2:10).

DO YOU KNOW THAT...

When you became a Christian the ownership of your life changes hands? In the past, you were the boss doing things the way you felt like...

In the past, the devil could toss you around, bending your life out of shape whenever he felt like, hindering your blessings whenever it pleased him...

Now, you have a new boss. You have received JESUS, and HE is now in charge. HE is the sole determiner of your destiny. HE is your Guide, your fortress, your shield, your help, your Deliverer. HE is your Christ. (Romans 10:9).

FREQUENTLY ASKED QUESTIONS

How to love yourself

How can I know that GOD has forgiven me?   (1 John 1: 8-9)

How can I know that I have eternal life?   (John 5:24)

How can I know that GOD is with me?   (John 6:37, Hebrews 13:5)

How can I know that GOD hears me?   (Jeremiah 29: 12-13)

DO YOU KNOW THAT...

You have access to divine power designed to bring victory, deliverance and prosperity into your life. You no longer need to be burdened by sin, sorrow and Satan.

You can be set free from curses, evil covenants, satanic embargoes, limitations and so on. All you need to do is move on the next stage, which is to submit yourself for proper deliverance in a Bible-believing church so that the shackles of Satan can be shattered forever out of your life, marriage, finances, career, health, academics and so on.

I want to hear from you, write me on abayendi@gmail.com

The author:

PROPHET ABRAHAM DOLLAR AYENDI

How to love yourself

An Apostolic Prophet, founder and general overseer of Zion Embassy (Christ church), a fast growing church Network with ministry branches in Ireland, South Africa, United Kingdom, Nigeria, Canada and Singapore. He is the C.E.O of Zion publishing house.

He is a dedicated Social Worker by training and a Community champion. Prophet Abraham as he is fondly called is also the founding president of www.yourfamilyfm.com, Family Fm (your Family community radio station 94.3) and the Principal of www.globalfamilyhealthcare.com headquartered in Dublin, Republic of Ireland.

An ardent Scholar, he holds a Post Graduate Diploma and a Masters degree in Social Care and Social Justice from Atlantic Technological University, Sligo, Republic of Ireland.
A revivalist and international conference speaker with divers signs and wonders following his ministrations.

A prolific writer and author of several books including:

- NEVER GIVE UP
- DON'T SETTLE FOR LESS
- YOU CAN SUCCEED
- THE POWER OF PRAYER
- QUIET TIME
- WATCHMAN
- NEW LIFE

How to love yourself

- HOW TO LOVE YOURSELF
- IN LOVE WITH GOD
- SINGLES MINGLES
- I WANT TO GET MARRIED
- HAPPILY MARRIED AFTER
- HOW TO KNOW HE LOVES YOU
- HOW DO I KNOW SHE LOVES ME
- TRUE LOVE
- PASTOR: YOU CAN SUCCEED.
- LETS TALK ABOUT SEX
- BEFORE I SAY I DO
- SINGLE AGAIN
- DEALING WITH DIVORCE
- CHILDREN IN DIVORCE
- OVERCOMING ANXIETY
- DEALING WITH DEPRESSION
- MAKING MONEY ONLINE
- HOW TO MAKE GOOD MONEY
- STARTING A BUSINESS
- DISCIPLINE
- MIRACLES NOW
- NO MORE INSTABILITY
- OVERCOMING GRIEF
- NEW DAD
- NEW MUM
- RAISING TEANAGE GIRLS
- RAISING TEANAGE BOYS
- RAISING GODLY CHILDREN
- FULFILLING YOUR CALLING
- HOW TO KNOW HE IS CHEATING
- HOW TO KNOW SHE IS CHEATING
- HOW TO BUILD MARRIAGE THAT WILL LAST FORVER
- HOW TO LOVE YOUR WIFE

How to love yourself

- SUBMISSION IN MARRIAGE
- HOW TO LOVE YOUR HUSBAND
- INVESTMENT BIBLE
- UNDERSTANDING WISDOM
- RADICAL FAITH
- MENTAL HEALTH

ABOUT THE AUTHOR

Abraham Dollar is a dedicated Social Worker by training and a Community champion. Prophet Abraham as he is fondly called is also the founding president of www.yourfamilyfm.com, Family Fm (your Family community radio station 94.3) and the Principal of www.globalfamilyhealthcare.com headquartered in Dublin, Republic of Ireland.

A revivalist and international conference speaker with divers signs and wonders following his ministrations.

How to love yourself

ABOUT THE AUTHOR

Abraham Dollar is a transformative preacher of the gospel, as well as the CEO of Zion Publishing House. With a background in social care work, he is a dedicated professional and a true community champion. Not only is he the founding president of Your Family FM (www.yourfamilyfm.com), a community radio station broadcasting on 94.3 FM, but he is also the principal of Global Family Healthcare (www.globalfamilyhealthcare.com), which is headquartered in Dublin, Republic of Ireland.

Abraham Dollar is an ardent scholar, having completed a Post Graduate Diploma and a Masters degree in Social Care and Social Justice from Atlantic Technological University in Sligo, Republic of Ireland. His commitment to academic excellence and his passion for addressing social issues shine through in his work.

As a revivalist and international conference speaker, Abraham Dollar's powerful ministry is accompanied by diverse signs and wonders. His profound ability to inspire and bring about positive change has captivated audiences around the world.

Abraham Dollar truly embodies the essence of a dedicated preacher, a social care professional, and a community leader. Through his various roles and accomplishments, he continues to make a significant impact on society and uplift those around him.

ABOUT THE BOOK

In a world where loving others at the detriment of oneself has become the norm, it's imperative to help you know that it's okay to Love yourself.

This is a book that will guide you on the journey to self-love while obeying the ultimate commandment "Love Your Neighbour as you love yourself.

ZION HOUSE PUBLISHING

Printed in Great Britain
by Amazon